LET'S INVESTIGATE SCIENCE
SCIENCE
The Environment

LET'S INVESTIGATE SCIENCE

The Environment

Robin Kerrod

Illustrated by Ted Evans

MARSHALL CAVENDISH
NEW YORK · LONDON · TORONTO · SYDNEY

Library Edition Published 1994

© Marshall Cavendish Corporation 1994

Published by Marshall Cavendish Corporation
2415 Jerusalem Avenue
PO Box 587
North Bellmore
New York 11710

Series created by Graham Beehag Book Design

Library of Congress Cataloging-in-Publication Data

Kerrod, Robin.
    The Environment / Robin Kerrod; llustrated by Ted Evans.
    p. cm. -- (Let's investigate science)
    Includes index.
    ISBN 1-85435-625-9 ISBN 1-85435-620-8 (set)
    1. Environmental education -- Juvenile literature. 2. Human
ecology -- Juvenile literature. 3. Environmental protection --
Juvenile literature. [1. Ecology. 2. Environmental protection.]
I. Evans, Ted ill. II. Title. III. Series: Kerrod, Robin. Let's
investigate science.
    GE115.K47 1994   93-8752
    383.7--dc20   CIP
                                           AC

MCC Editorial Consultant: Marvin Tolman, Ed.D.
                    Brigham Young University

Printed and bound in Hong Kong

Contents

Introduction

The environment means our surroundings. Today, we are talking about and thinking about the environment more than ever before. This is because we are becoming aware that our modern way of life is posing an increasing threat to it. The threat is not just to our immediate environment – where we live – but also to the environment of the whole Earth.

People once thought that they could do anything they liked to the Earth, and the Earth would not be affected. They could burn lots of gas in car engines, discharge wastes into rivers, cut down as many trees as they liked, and so on, and the Earth would cope. So they thought. But we know now that the Earth can't cope. Fumes from burning gas and wastes, discharged from sewage works and factories, are among the many things in the modern world that are causing serious pollution, or poisoning, of the environment.

In this book we look at the way nature and humans have shaped our environment. We highlight some of the pressing environmental problems that we now face, and look at ways of solving them.

You can check your answers to the questions featured throughout this book on pages 60-61.

◄ **Photographs of the Earth taken from space made people realize just how precious and fragile our world is. This has led to the idea of "Spaceship Earth" – Earth as a unique spaceship carrying life through the Universe. We know of no other body that has life of any kind.**

1 The Natural Environment

◀ Yosemite Falls, pictured here framed by tall conifer trees. The Falls are in Yosemite National Park in the Sierra Nevada Mountains of California. Flowing water is one of the main natural shapers of the landscape.

Q 1. The picture was taken in July. Would the flow of water over the Falls be lesser or greater in May; or in September?

Left to itself, nature creates its own environment. We can think of this as being made up of two parts. First there is the physical environment – the land, the water, the air, and the climate. Then there is the biological, or living environment, which consists of plants and animals.

The physical environment is always changing, but usually so slowly that we don't notice. It changes because of forces such as the action of the weather, the pounding of the waves on the seashore, and the sandblasting action of wind-blown sand.

The living environment is a fascinating one. In any location, plants and animals live together in a community. Each species (kind) of living things interacts with the others around it in one way or another, creating a settled, or stable, environment. We often call this the balance of nature. Problems are created if this balance is upset.

▼ Beavers can change the landscape dramatically. They fell trees to provide materials to build their lodges (homes) and dams.

Q 2. Why do beavers build dams?

The physical environment

This is the non-living, or inorganic, part of our surroundings. It is the substance of which our world is made up.

We can divide our physical environment into three parts. There is the rocky part, which makes up the ground under our feet and the surrounding landscape. This is sometimes called the lithosphere, from the Greek word "lithos," meaning stone. There is the watery part, made up of the rivers, lakes, and the oceans. This is often called the hydrosphere. Then there is the gassy part, made up of the air all around us, or the atmosphere.

A certain amount of water shuttles back and forth between the hydrosphere and the atmosphere all the time, in a never-ending process called the water cycle. This plays a leading role in determining another very important aspect of the physical environment – the weather. The other main factor that affects the weather is the heat received from the Sun.

The amount of solar (Sun) heat received in a given place varies throughout the world, with areas near the Equator receiving most heat, and places near the Poles receiving the least. This results in different climates throughout the world. The climate of a region is one of the major factors in determining what kind of living environment is found there (see page 16).

▶▶ Russet-colored clouds in the dawn sky. Clouds are made up of tiny droplets of water or ice crystals. They form when air carrying water vapor cools high up in the atmosphere.

▼ Oceans cover more than two-thirds of the Earth's surface. They are filled with the chemical hydrogen oxide, or water.

Q If H is hydrogen and O is oxygen, what is water?

▶▶ A view from space of the Himalaya mountains. The solid crust of the Earth is made up of rock and in places has wrinkled, creating mountain ranges. Over much of the land area, the bedrock is covered with soil, made up of bits of worn-away rocks, together with organic matter from rotted plants and animals.

◀ Rocks are made up of minerals. When they have space to grow, minerals form crystals like this.

10

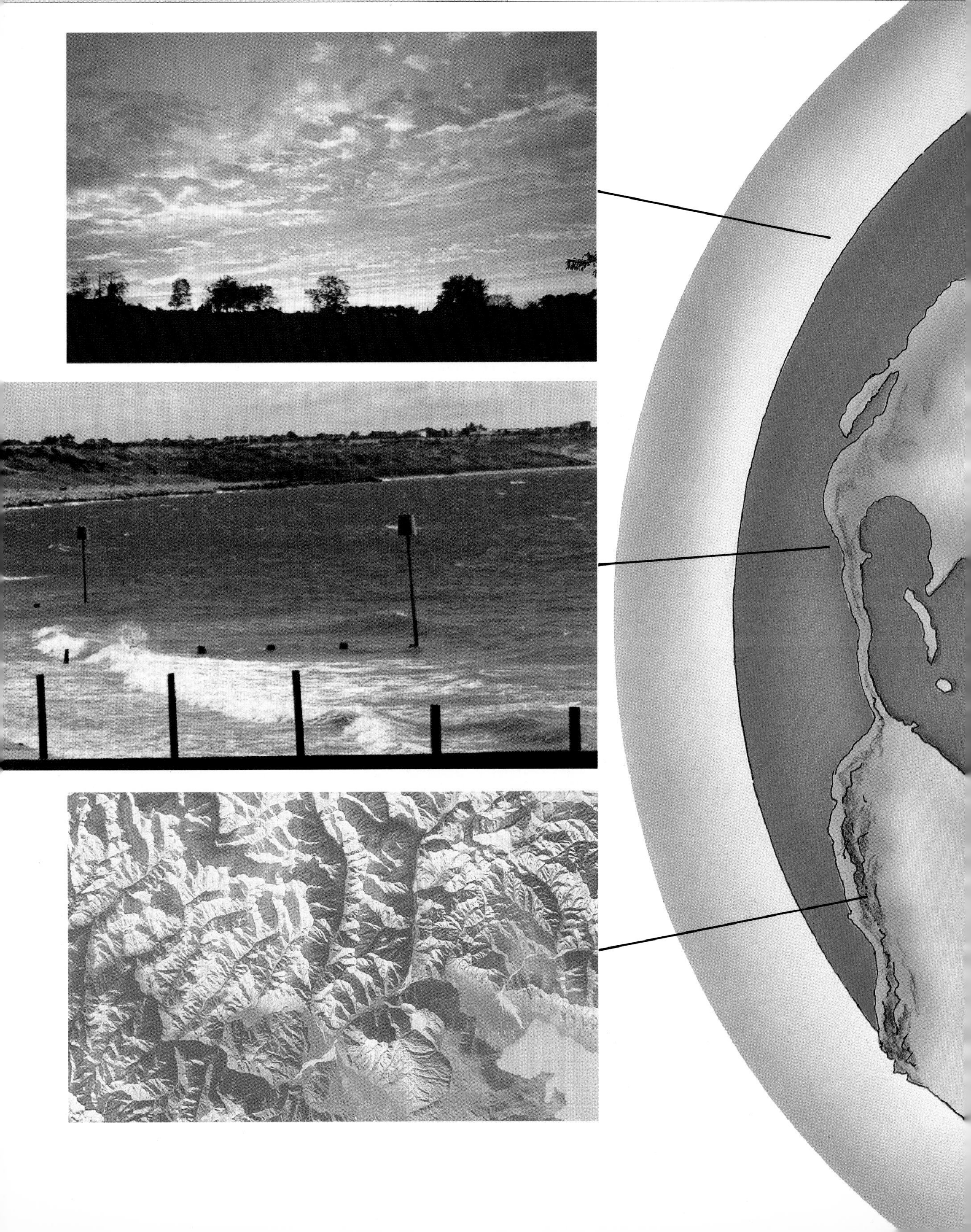

IT'S AMAZING!

200 million years ago all the land mass of the world was joined together, forming a supercontinent known as Pangaea. Then this supercontinent began to split up. The continents started "drifting" because of movements in the Earth's upper layer, or crust. Continental drift is still going on today.

▼ The Grand Canyon in Arizona appears to have changed little since it was first studied closely in the early 1800s. Weathering and erosion by the Colorado River has been gradually altering the shape of this outstanding natural wonder of the world, born millions of years ago.

The changing landscape

Natural forces are constantly changing the face of the Earth. Usually the process is so gradual that we can see little change from year to year. But over maybe 10 years, half a century or a century, noticeable changes will take place.

One of the major forces shaping the landscape is running water. Swift-flowing streams and rivers gradually wear away the rocks and soil they run over. The pounding of the ocean waves on the shore is also a powerful shaping force. The wearing away of the landscape by water is one example of erosion.

Under the weather

There are many other natural forces that bring about erosion. Frost is one. When water runs into cracks in rocks and there is a frost, the water turns to ice. As it does so, it expands and exerts tremendous pressure on the rocks, eventually splitting them. At the bottom of cliffs you often see large deposits of rocky material split off the rock face in this way.

The action of frost on rocks is an example of what is called weathering, the erosion of the landscape by the weather.

In permanently cold regions, the falling snow packs down into ice. This often happens in high mountain valleys. Eventually the weight of the ice causes it to start moving, slowly, downhill. It becomes a river of ice. Stones embedded in the ice grind away the sides and the floor of the valley.

Q What do we call such a "river of ice?"

Sandblasting

The wind is another weathering agent. It is one of the main forces of erosion in desert regions. When the wind blows strongly, it picks up fine particles of sand. As the wind blows against the rocks, the particles are hurled against them, and wear them away by a grinding action.

Weathering can also be chemical. For example, when rainwater containing traces of acid runs over the rocks, it starts to dissolve them. This often creates caves, particularly in limestone rocks.

◀ The sea constantly attacks the rocks along its shores, wearing them away. Sometimes this results in the formation of natural arches like this. But it will not be long before the sea eats deeper into the rocks and the arch collapses.

Sudden change

As a rule, natural agents of change such as erosion alter the physical environment quite slowly. But on occasion, nature unleashes unbelievable violence that changes the environment very rapidly indeed.

This happens, for example, during hurricanes, tropical storms in which winds spiral round a calm "eye" at speeds of up to 150 mph (240 km/h). Hurricane Andrew, which hit Florida and Louisiana in August 1992, was one of the most destructive of recent times, devastating large areas and making 160,000 people homeless. Many Americans are also unfortunately familiar with "twisters" – violent spiralling windstorms that can toss cars and trailers about like confetti.

Q What is the proper name for a twister?

Great eruptions

Usually, storms affect the living environment more than the physical one and for a relatively short period. But other agents of sudden change alter the landscape dramatically and permanently.

None are more dramatic than volcanoes. They erupt, usually without warning, and pour molten lava over the surrounding landscape. The lava cools and sets into rock. Many volcanoes billow out great clouds of ash for months. Most of this falls to the ground locally, but much rises high

▼ **This street looks almost exactly as it did nearly 2,000 years ago when it was built. It is in an ancient Roman city called Herculaneum, just outside Naples, Italy. In the year AD 79 the nearby volcano Vesuvius erupted and buried the city under lava and ash, which preserved it exactly as it was.**

◄ **The famous Meteor Crater in Arizona, over 1,380 yards (1,260 meters) across, shows that some agents of change are out of this world. The Crater was made by a huge meteorite, which slammed into the Earth tens of thousands of years ago. Such a body hitting a big city today would totally destroy it and send masses of dust and debris into the air. This could have the same effect as volcanic ash and bring about global cooling.**

14

into the atmosphere and in time is carried all around the world. The ash has a marked effect on the environment. Locally, it covers vegetation and chokes streams. The high-level ash, however, may affect the whole global environment. The particles form a kind of sunshield around the Earth that partly blocks the Sun's rays. This has the effect of cooling the entire climate on Earth. The ash-rich eruption of Mt. Pinatubo in the Philippines in 1991 brought about significant global cooling over the next few years.

Earthquakes are another terrifying example of how nature can alter the landscape. They occur when sections of the Earth's crust suddenly move. The ground shakes violently, heaves up and down and often splits apart. The tremors occur only for a few seconds, but with enough force to topple homes and office blocks as though they were made of matchsticks.

15

▼ **The eruption of Mt. Pinatubo on the Philippine island of Luzon threw billions of cubic yards of ash into the air. The volcano literally "blew its top" in June 1991, creating a crater 1½ miles (2 km) in diameter.**

The living environment

Life exists on Earth in extraordinary rich variety, from microscopic water plants you need a microscope to see, to Blue whales 100 feet (31 meters) long and weighing 210 tons (190 tonnes). In all there may be as many as 30 million different species (kinds) of plants and animals on Earth at the present time. We haven't even discovered most yet! Only about 2 million have been discovered and described.

Every living thing is happiest in a particular kind of place, where the temperature, moisture and environment in general is just right for it. We call this its habitat. A particular habitat will attract a number of plants and animals, and together they will form a natural community. The study of plants and animals in their natural habitats and the relationships between them is called ecology.

16

In an oak tree

A tree can be a community all by itself. A mature oak tree, for example, can be the home of as many as 200 different

▼ **Some of the residents that live in an oak tree. At any one time the tree could be the home of tens of thousands of individual creatures.**

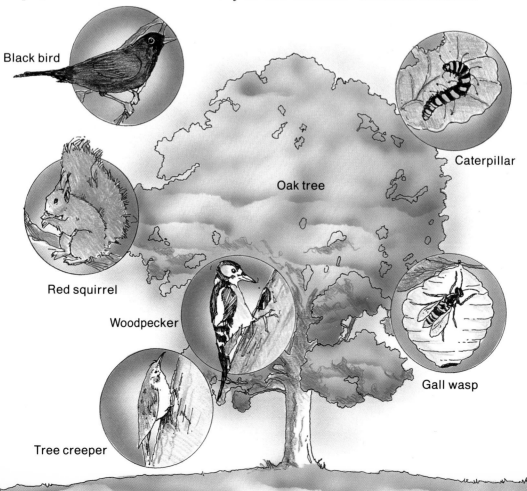

Black bird

Caterpillar

Oak tree

Red squirrel

Woodpecker

Gall wasp

Tree creeper

Lizard

Flamingoes

Spider monkey

Polar bear

species of insects alone, and it can carry tens of thousands of each one. The oak leaves provide food for the larvae (caterpillars) of the insects, which include various flies, moths and beetles. One interesting oak-tree insect is the gall wasp, whose larvae cause the growth of round galls, or "oak apples." The insects themselves provide food for other creatures, such as spiders and woodland birds like tits. Acorns from the tree provide food for squirrels, which may also nest in the branches. Holes in the trunk provide homes for woodpeckers.

Special relationships

The species in a community are usually linked together by a food chain (see page 18). But sometimes they take part in quite a different kind of relationship. The Crocodile bird, for example, hops in and out of the crocodile's mouth, picking bits of food from between the teeth, without coming to any harm. The crocodile somehow knows that the bird is helping to keep its teeth clean and doesn't attack!

Q Plants and animals can have close relationships, too. Bees and other insects have a close relationship with flowering plants. What is it?

A large number of different habitats occur on Earth. Among the most important features of a habitat are the temperature and the presence or absence of water. The flamingo is happiest in the warm wetlands. Lizards, being cold-blooded creatures, prefer hot climates. Spider monkeys like the lush habitat of the tropical rain forest. Polar bears, however, prefer the snow-covered regions near the North Pole.

17

Chains, webs and pyramids

In order to stay alive, every living thing needs food. For animals, searching for food and eating are the most important things they do, and in general these things occupy much, if not most, of their time. Finding a mate and raising young is another driving force in an animal's life, for they must reproduce or have offspring if their kind is to survive. All the while, they must also be on the lookout for other animals that could harm them or their family group.

Finding food

Green plants do not have to go looking for food because they make their own. Using the energy in sunlight, they make their food from substances they take up from the ground and absorb from the air. The process is called photosynthesis.

Plants take in carbon dioxide from the air and combine it with water from the soil to make simple sugars. They use some of this food themselves and store the surplus in their tissues.

Animals can't make their own food and, directly or indirectly, have to get their food from plants. Animals such as antelopes, horses, and cattle eat plants directly for food. We call them herbivores. Other animals, called carnivores, get their food by eating the herbivores.

In a particular community, food chains link the plants and animals. On the African plains, for example: antelope feed on the grass, and lions feed on antelope. Lion – antelope – grass is an example of a simple food chain. In practice many such chains exist in a community. For example, antelope are also preyed upon by cheetahs. Their carcasses also provide food for hyenas and vultures. So the various food chains are connected. They can be brought together to form a much more complicated network called a food web. Food chains and food webs are basic features of the living environment and determine the balance between the numbers of the different species involved.

A food pyramid among the bird life in a typical woodland. There may be only one pair of hawks, which prey on larger numbers of smaller birds, which prey on thousands of insects as adults or caterpillars.

18

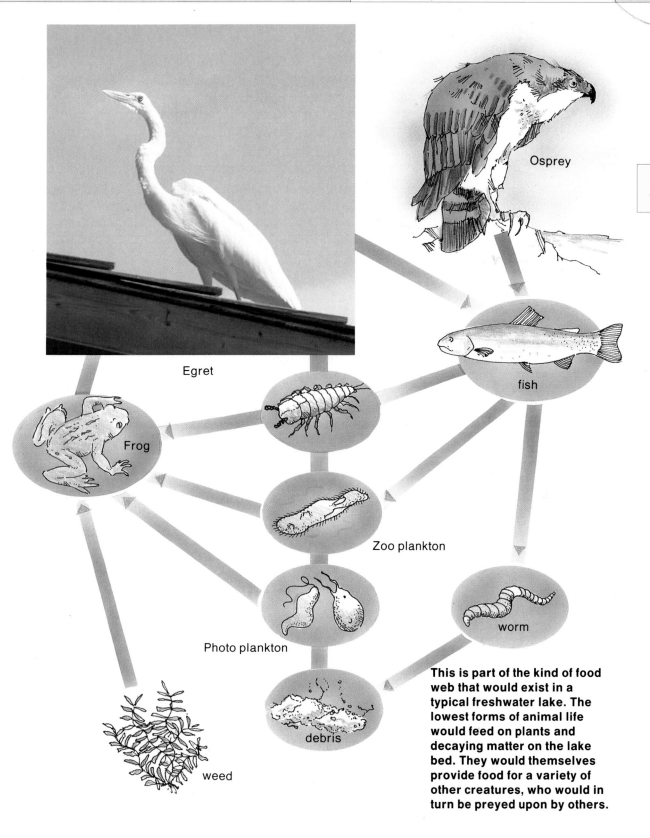

Osprey

Egret

fish

Frog

Zoo plankton

Photo plankton

worm

debris

weed

This is part of the kind of food web that would exist in a typical freshwater lake. The lowest forms of animal life would feed on plants and decaying matter on the lake bed. They would themselves provide food for a variety of other creatures, who would in turn be preyed upon by others.

Extinctions

There has been some kind of life on our planet for maybe as long as 3 billion years. Scientists have found traces of tiny bacteria in rocks of this age. But a great "explosion" of life did not occur until about 500-590 million years ago, during a time in Earth's history called the Cambrian Period.

Since then, we have been able to trace the evolution, or development, of life on Earth through the remains, or fossils, they left behind.

The fossil record shows how over hundreds of millions of years different plants and animals have appeared, perhaps changed, and then disappeared off the face of the Earth.

Such disappearances are called extinctions. Usually, a species dwindles in numbers over a long period before it finally disappears. But sometimes a species – sometimes many species together – will disappear suddenly.

▲ An ammonite fossil. Ammonites flourished in the oceans for more than 300 million years. They disappeared suddenly about 65 million years ago.

▼ The dinosaurs ruled the Earth for 100 million years, not only on land but also in the water and in the air. The large dinosaur here is Triceratops, a 9-ton (8-tonne) monster about 25 feet (8 meters) long. It was a plant-eater that died out suddenly, with all the other dinosaurs, about 65 million years ago.

The slow extinctions were probably caused by gradual changes in climate or the rise of more dominant life forms. But the sudden extinctions still remain something of a mystery. One explanation is that they were triggered by a catastrophe such as the impact of a huge meteorite from outer space (see page 15).

In more recent times, sudden extinctions have been brought about by our own species. The dodo and the North American passenger pigeon are classic examples of this. Thousands of wildlife species – both plants and animals – are now at risk because of human activities, as we shall see in the next chapter.

▼ **The ill-fated passenger pigeon. In the early 1800s eastern North America had a pigeon population that numbered in the billions. When the pigeons migrated, they would darken the skies for days. But they were slaughtered for food to such an extent that by 1916 they were extinct. The last ever passenger pigeon died in Cincinnati zoo.**

▼ **This saber-toothed tiger was a formidable predator, which was around at the same time as the mammoth. Its bones have been found in the La Brea tar pits in Los Angeles.**

▶ **The dodo was a large flightless bird that lived on the island of Mauritius, in the Indian Ocean. European settlers and sailors found it an easy source of food. It became extinct in about 1680, after being known to humans for only about a century.**

2

The Man-made Environment

◀ **Boston at night. The city provides a typical urban environment of buildings, streets and sidewalks that is totally man-made and unnatural. When night falls, millions of electric lamps bring artificial daylight to the city, enabling the human population to extend the natural day for work and leisure.**

Human beings started to alter the natural environment when they first became farmers, about 10,000 years ago. They began cutting down trees and clearing the land to plant crops. Farming has been shaping the landscape ever since.

But modern farming methods can pose a much more serious threat to the environment. If too many chemicals are used, they can cause serious pollution and harm wildlife.

Another age-old activity, mining, can also have a marked effect on the landscape. But often it is the materials mined, such as fuels, that affect the environment more.

Coal, for example, creates serious air pollution when it burns. It produces fumes and gases that give rise to acid rain and promote global warming. Acid rain and global warming cause many of the most serious environmental problems confronting the world today.

▶ **Huge bucket-wheel excavators like this are among the gigantic machines that change the face of the Earth in mining operations.**

People

Over the past two to three million years, the animal species *Homo sapiens* has become the dominant life form on Earth. *Homo sapiens* is the human species, to which all races of mankind belong.

It is the sheer success of our species that is the underlying cause of most of the environmental problems we face today. Agriculture's success in forcing nature to be ever more productive has produced enough food to feed an expanding population. Success in medicine has kept many from dying of diseases that once would have been fatal and has also allowed people to live much longer than ever before.

As a result, the world's population has risen beyond natural limits, and is still rising. The population at present is over 5 billion, and by the year 2070 it might be double that figure.

This population explosion puts humankind in direct conflict with nature. The need for extra land to grow food, to extract minerals, to dispose of wastes, and to provide shelter threatens wild plants and animals above all by destroying their habitats.

Q The human population is increasing rapidly. It is estimated that every four seconds, ten babies are born into the world. How many babies is this a year?

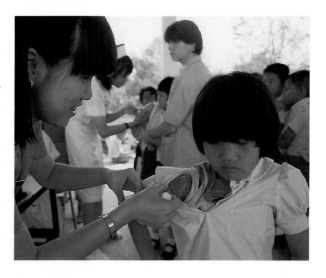

▲ A child being innoculated against disease. The innoculation will help her body build up natural immunity (resistance) to the disease, so that if she is exposed to it later in life, she will not be affected. Immunization has greatly improved the health of the world's population.

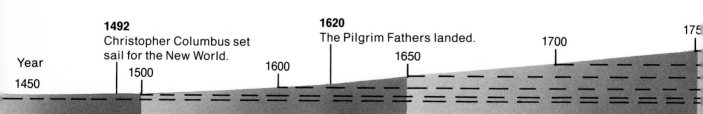

Year
1450

1492
Christopher Columbus set sail for the New World.
1500

1600

1620
The Pilgrim Fathers landed.
1650

1700

175

◄ Although most industrialized countries have a food surplus, millions of people in underdeveloped countries are starving. This is happening because of drought, failed crops and local wars, which often prevent aid getting through to the starving people.

INVESTIGATE

Find out from government records in your local library what the birth rate is now in your state and in the U.S. overall. Compare this with the death rate. Then work out the rate of increase in population.

▼ This graph shows the way inwhich the world population has increased over the past 500 years. When Columbus set out for the New World, the population was less than half a billion. The population began rising sharply inthe 1800s during the period of industrial expansion known as the Industrial Revolution.

1969
Apollo 11 astronaut Neil Armstrong set foot on the Moon.

2000

1950

1939
World War 2 began; lasted until 1945 in Europe, 1946 in Pacific.

1914
World War 1 began; lasted until 1918.

1861
Civil War began; lasted until 1865.

1900

1776
Declaration of Independence.

1850

1800

Billion people

7
6
5
4
3
2
1
0

26

The cultivation of two different kinds of cereals in two different parts of the world has led to two very different landscapes. In North America (above), the crop is wheat, and it is grown in huge fields. In South-east Asia (below), the crop is rice, and it is grown in small terraced "paddies," which are periodically flooded.

Farming

Wherever human beings settle on Earth, they alter the living environment around them in one way or another. Mostly they alter it by farming so that they can produce food and other materials they need. They clear out native species of plants and animals and introduce plants (crops) and animals (livestock) of their own.

The most important crops farmers grow are cereals, such as wheat, corn, and rice. The most important livestock are cattle, hogs, and sheep. Crop farming has shaped the landscape dramatically, and nowhere more so than on the vast prairie land of North America, which is close to being one continuous field. Wheat is the main crop grown there.

Q The U.S. produces about 83 million tons (75 million tonnes) of wheat a year, which is 12.5 percent of the world total. How much wheat does the world produce a year?

Chemical cultivation

On a modern farm, the same crop is usually planted in the same field, year after year. By itself, such a method of cultivation would soon remove all the nutrients (nourishing substances) from the soil. It would also allow the diseases and pests that attack that particular crop to flourish.

To keep their fields productive, farmers resort to chemical weapons. They apply fertilizers to enrich the soil, and spray the crops with pesticides to kill insects and other pests and with fungicides to kill fungus diseases. They also apply chemicals called herbicides to kill weeds. The problem with all these chemicals is that they can do serious harm to the environment. Nitrate and phosphate fertilizers can run off the land and cause water pollution (see page 40). Many pesticides not only kill pests but harm other wildlife as well.

▼ Applying fungicide by a tractor-mounted spray boom.

27

The chemical "dressing" applied to seeds has been responsible for widespread damage to wildlife, especially to animals at the top of the food chain. This is because of the way poisons build up in the chain. For example, mice and small birds eat the chemically coated seeds. The chemical poison gradually builds up in their body tissues. So when a predator such as a hawk, kills and feeds on mice and birds, he receives more concentrated doses of poison.

Forests

Thick forests once covered much of the Earth's surface. But over the past 10,000 years or so, most of them have been cut down to provide space for human beings to settle and farm. Only two large expanses, or "belts," of forest remain.

One is the northern forest belt in the far north of North America, Europe, and Asia. Its typical trees are evergreen conifers ("cone-bearers"), with needle-like leaves. They have relatively soft wood. The other remaining forest region is the tropical rain forest belt, which spans the Equator. Its typical trees are also evergreen but have broad leaves and hard wood.

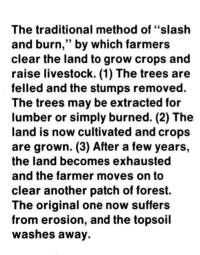

1.

2.

The traditional method of "slash and burn," by which farmers clear the land to grow crops and raise livestock. (1) The trees are felled and the stumps removed. The trees may be extracted for lumber or simply burned. (2) The land is now cultivated and crops are grown. (3) After a few years, the land becomes exhausted and the farmer moves on to clear another patch of forest. The original one now suffers from erosion, and the topsoil washes away.

Destroying the forests

The northern conifer forests are being cut down mainly for lumber and for making into woodpulp and paper. The tropical forests are being cut down partly for their lumber, but mainly to clear land for farming. Most of them happen to be in underdeveloped countries, whose people regard them as a resource to be exploited as much as possible in order to improve their way of life.

The problem is the vast scale on which this tropical forest clearance is happening. Every year, in South America, Africa, and Southeast Asia, some 40 million acres (16 million hectares) of tropical forest is being destroyed. This is an area the size of New England! At this rate, the tropical forests could disappear completely in less than 50 years.

Environmental catastrophe

Tropical forest destruction is one of the biggest threats there is to the environment. These forests are the richest habitats on Earth for both animal and plant life. They contain at least half of all living species, most of which have not yet been discovered.

Another worrying aspect of forest destruction is the effect it might have on the atmosphere. The forests act as part of the "lungs" of the world, taking in carbon dioxide and giving out oxygen. Without them, the proportion of carbon dioxide in the air must rise, increasing the greenhouse effect (see page 37).

29

3.

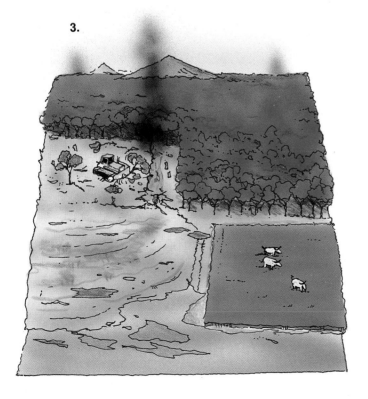

▼ Foresters transplant conifer seedlings raised on a nursery plot into their final growing positions in a new forest region. In the United states and other developed countries, new forests are planted to replace those cut down in logging operations.

Mining

Farming and forestry provide some of our raw materials –
the materials we need to make things. But we get most
of our raw materials from the ground by mining. Mining
provides us with coal and with minerals, which we can
then process into useful products.

The most important of these products are metals. Without metals, we would still be living in the Stone Age. We
call the minerals that we can process into metals "ores."
By far the most important metal is iron, which we use
mainly in the form of its alloy, steel. Every year the U.S.
alone extracts something like 110 million tons (100 million
tonnes) of iron ore from the ground. This is part of the 55
billion tons (50 billion tonnes) of minerals the world extracts each year.

30

▼ **This great hole in the ground, 2,600 feet (800 meters) deep, is the famous Bingham Canyon copper mine, which is located about 30 miles (50 km) southwest of Salt Lake City, Utah. About 3.5 billion tons (3.2 billion tonnes) of ore were removed between January 1, 1906, and December 31, 1992.**

Q **On average, how many tons (tonnes) of ore have been produced per day?**

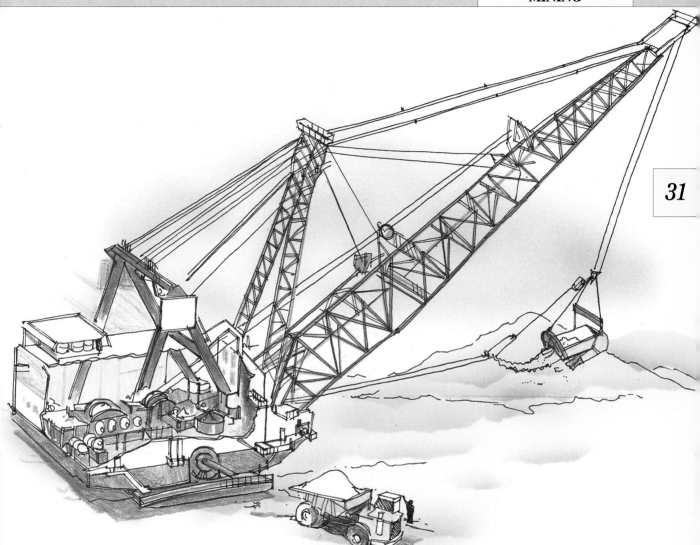

Most iron ore is mined from pits at the surface, a method known as open-pit, or opencast mining. Most coal and many materials, including copper and aluminum ores, are mined in the same way. Others, including nickel , lead, and zinc ores, and more coal, are mined underground. Open-pit mining affects the environment the most. It causes a permanent scar on the landscape, and produces dust that blankets the countryside. Where explosives are used to break up the rocks, this disturbs the wildlife.

We are using up our minerals very rapidly, and early next century, many existing mines will start to run out. This will mean that mining geologists will have to find alternative sites for mines, which will put even greater pressure on the environment.

▲ **Mammoth excavators like this can be seen at work at open-pit mines, where they are used to strip off any dirt covering the mineral deposit. The metal "boom" on this machine is nearly 100 yards (meters) long. Its bucket can scoop up over 75 cubic yards (60 cubic meters) of soil at one bite!**

◄ The Trans-Alaskan Pipeline snakes through the Alaskan wilderness, seen here during the brief summer. Construction of the 800-mile (1,285-km) long pipeline through an hitherto untouched landscape encountered many difficult problems including permafrost, caribou, and earthquakes.

Permafrost is the permanently frozen ground beneath the surface, which doesn't melt even in summer. So where there was permafrost, the pipeline had to be raised above ground, as in this picture. If the pipeline had been buried, the warm oil running through the pipe would have melted the permafrost and given rise to severe erosion. The pipeline also crosses three earthquake zones. In these areas it is supported on special mountings that are able to move several feet up and down and from side to side. This should prevent the pipeline breaking if an earthquake does occur.

►► The New York skyline is dominated by masterpieces of construction, buildings that literally seem to "scrape the sky." The twin towers of the World Trade Center soar to more than a quarter-of-a-mile (402 meters) high. The sidewalks and streets of New York make up the typical urban landscape of a big city, the so-called concrete jungle, in which the natural environment is limited to oases like Central Park.

Engineering the landscape

The activities of the mining engineer ruin the natural landscape, but usually only over a relatively small area. The activities of the civil engineer can alter the landscape and the environment over a much wider area.

Civil engineers are the people who build roads, dams, canals, bridges, and tunnels. Their work generally involves shifting vast amounts of surface rock and soil, material often termed "muck." In constructing the New Cornelia Tailings Dam in Arizona, for example, engineers shifted more than 260 million cubic yards (200 million cubic meters) of muck.

But often the greatest environmental impact of dam construction is caused by the flooding of the land behind the dam to create the reservoir. In the case of the Itaipu Dam across the Parana River in South America, the flooding destroyed thousands of square kilometers of tropical forest and displaced 40,000 people.

The construction of roads also destroys natural habitats, and brings with it the threat of pollution. But sometimes the roadsides become sancturies for wild flowers and small animals, because they are not usually sprayed with chemicals.

▲ The urban landscape of Detroit (upper half) from the air. It is photographed on infrared film, on which deep red shows vegetation, and grays concrete and other man-made materials. The criss-cross network of city streets is clearly evident. The prominent gray lines indicate the multilane freeways.

Polluting the air

We and most other living things must breathe in air to stay alive. Over the past 200 years, the air about us has been getting increasingly polluted. The process began during the rapid expansion of industry we call the Industrial Revolution and has gotten gradually worse and worse.

One of the main causes of air pollution is the burning of fossil fuels, particularly coal. Today, power stations are among the worst offenders, along with factories. When the fuel burns in their furnaces, smoke and fumes are given off into the atmosphere. Among the fumes is the gas sulfur dioxide, which has a sharp, choking smell.

In the atmosphere, sulfur dioxide combines with the oxygen in the air and droplets of moisture to form sulfuric acid. Then, when the droplets get big enough, they fall as acid rain.

Exhaust fumes

Over the last 100 years or so another polluter has appeared on the scene in ever increasing numbers – the motor

34

INVESTIGATE

To see what effect acid rain has on limestone, find a piece of chalk, which is chemically the same as limestone. Scrape off some of the chalk into a glass and add a little vinegar, which is an acid. What happens?

▼ Power stations that burn coal are among the worst air polluters. This is because most coal contains sulfur, which is one of the main causes of acid rain.

vehicle. The millions of cars, trucks, and buses on our roads burn mainly gasoline, and give off all kinds of poisonous fumes in their exhausts. Among them are nitrogen oxides. They are another cause of acid rain because they change into nitric acid in the air. Some of the older cars, which use regular gasoline, release another pollutant into the air – lead.

The effects of acid rain can be devastating to the environment. It attacks trees and other plants it falls on – many of the great forest regions in North America and northern Europe are already badly affected. Acid rain also runs off into rivers and lakes, and upsets their natural chemical balance. This in time kills off the water plants, fish, and other aquatic life.

Q Lakes are particularly affected by acid rain. Why?

IT'S AMAZING!

Mexico City, with its 8½ million people and tens of thousands of cars, is one of the world's most polluted cities. When pollution is particularly bad, birds have been known to drop dead out of the sky.

35

▼ The effects of acid rain can be felt far away from the industrial centers that caused it. Many of the lakes and forests in the wilderness areas of North America are suffering.

Smog and the greenhouse

People who live in some big cities, especially Los Angeles, may be familiar with another form of air pollution caused mainly by the exhaust fumes from motor vehicles – a smoky fog we call smog. When smog is bad, people with breathing difficulties are seriously affected.

Smog occurs when the exhaust fumes get trapped by an upper layer of air, which prevents the normal circulation of the atmosphere. This happens particularly in certain natural basins, as in the Los Angeles area. When sunlight acts on the trapped fumes, harmful substances are produced, causing the smog.

36

All kinds of human activity produce greenhouse gases. Motor vehicles that burn gasoline and diesel fuel produce vast quantities, as do power stations and factories that burn coal, oil, and gas. Even modern farming plays its part, because cattle produce methane in their gut as they digest their food.

Greenhouse gases

Motor vehicles also give out large amounts of carbon dioxide in their exhaust fumes. This gas is in fact given out when any fuel – coal, oil, gas, or wood – burns in the air. So much carbon dioxide is now being released that it is helping to turn the atmosphere into a kind of greenhouse. A greenhouse works by trapping the Sun's energy, and that is what the carbon dioxide does. This greenhouse effect is slowly but surely causing the temperature of the Earth to rise. We call this global warming.

In time, global warming will change the pattern of climates all over the world. It will affect farming, it may cause more desert regions to form, and it may cause the ice caps to melt at the North and South Poles. If this happens, the oceans will rise, and many countries will be flooded.

Carbon dioxide is not the only gas that is bringing about the greenhouse effect. Methane and the substances called CFCs (see page 39) are doing so as well. Methane, which is the main gas in natural gas, is produced in large quantities by rotting vegetation in garbage dumps.

▲ A layer of smog settled over the city of Santiago, capital of Chile, in South America. The motor vehicles that jam the city streets are mostly to blame. The action of sunlight on the exhaust fumes creates gases that irritate the throat and cause breathing problems.

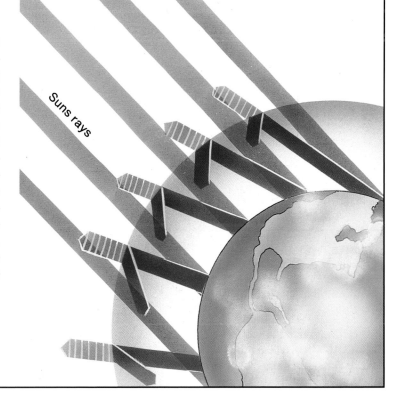

The greenhouse effect

The greenhouse effect occurs when gases in the atmosphere trap energy coming from the Sun. The Sun's rays carry solar energy to the ground. The ground heats up and itself gives off heat radiation (rays). The greenhouse gases in the atmosphere absorb some of the radiation, and the rest escapes into space. As the greenhouse gases build up, they absorb more and more heat, causing the atmosphere to warm up.

Suns rays

▲ An aerosol can, which uses a gas called a propellant to force out a spray of liquid.

The ozone hole

The Sun gives out energy not only as light and heat, but also invisible rays, such as gamma rays, X-rays, and ultraviolet rays. Fortunately, most of these rays are blocked by the atmosphere. It is fortunate because in large doses, they are harmful to all forms of life. The atmosphere does, however, let through some ultraviolet rays – they are the rays that tan you and sometimes burn you if you stay in the Sun too long.

The part of the atmosphere that filters out most of the ultraviolet rays is called the ozone layer. It is composed of the gas ozone, which is a form of oxygen. The layer occupies most of the part of the Earth's atmosphere we call the stratosphere, between about 10 and 30 miles (16 and 50 km) high.

Q 1. On Earth, where are X-rays used, and what are they used for?

Ozone destroyers

In the mid-1980s a NASA satellite checking the ozone layer reported that it was thinning dramatically over Antarctica, around the South Pole. Scientists spoke of this as an "ozone hole." Ozone holes have appeared over Antarctica regularly

ozone layer

Suns rays

▶ A layer of ozone in the Earth's atmosphere filters out most of the burning rays that come from the Sun.

Q 2. The picture is not drawn to scale. If it were, would the edge of the atmosphere be closer to the Earth or farther away?

ever since. They are now appearing in parts of the Northern Hemisphere, too.

A permanent thinning of the ozone layer would be bad news for all life on Earth, for it would lead to more ultraviolet radiation reaching the ground. People would be more easily burned when they ventured into sunlight and would also be more likely to get skin cancer. The stronger radiation might also be harmful to the plants we and other animals need as food.

Increased air pollution is what causes ozone holes. The main offending gases are called CFCs, or chlorofluorocarbons (carbon compounds containing chlorine and fluorine). These gases get into the atmosphere in various ways. For example, they may come from aerosol spray cans, which use them as propellants. They may come from refrigerators, which use them as the cooling liquid and vapor. They may also come from the manufacture of plastic foams.

To reduce the problem, the U.S. has banned the use of CFCs in spray cans and is phasing out CFCs in refrigerators. But there is still a worldwide problem because many countries have not followed suit.

▲ Sunbathers soak up the Sun's rays on Bondi Beach, Australia, letting them tan their skin. To be safe, sunbathers should always put on a sunblock cream to filter out the ultraviolet rays. This will become increasingly necessary if the ozone layer starts to thin.

◄ A NASA scientist examines a picture that shows levels of ozone in the Southern Hemisphere in 1987, when the biggest-ever "hole" was recorded near the South Pole.

IT'S AMAZING!

Not so long ago, some of the rivers running into the Great Lakes were so polluted that they often caught fire!

▼ Some of the main sources of water pollution. Factories produce all kinds of chemical wastes. Many towns discharge raw or partly treated sewage. Fertilizers run off the land in rainwater in agricultural areas. Oil gets into the seas when pipes leak and when ships clean out their fuel tanks or run aground.

Polluting the waters

Every day the world pours into its rivers and seas a frightening amount of poisonous substances. It was once thought that there was so much water on Earth that it could absorb any amount of waste and not be affected. But this is not true. Many rivers and lakes in countries throughout the world are dead or dying because of pollution. Lakes are especially at risk because they are enclosed bodies of water, and waste products build up in them.

Chemical pollutants

Chemical factories produce many toxic (poisonous) waste products. Some of the most harmful are compounds called chlorinated hydrocarbons. They are chemicals containing chlorine that are made from oil. They are related to substances used as pesticides (see page 26). Like pesticides, they do not break down easily. They enter the food chain (See page 18) when they are taken in by living things and build up in their tissues. All members of the food chain are affected. The higher up the chain an animal is, the more it will be affected.

Q Why are animals higher up the food chain more affected than those lower down?

town

river

petrochemical plant

garbage dump

raw sewage

toxic run off

spraying

Oil spills

Even in the oceans, toxic chemicals are also building up to dangerous levels. But the worst pollution at sea occurs when oil tankers are involved in collisions or when they run aground on rocks. When this happens and their hulls are split open, literally millions of gallons of oil can escape from them. It fouls the water and the beaches and all the wildlife on them. It can take many years before the environment and wildlife populations can recover.

Alaska wildlife was dealt a terrible blow when the supertanker *Exxon Valdez* ran aground in Prince William Sound in March 1989. It spilled over 11 million gallons (42 million liters) into the sea. The oil gradually spread over 1,100 miles (1,800 km) of coastline. Among the shorelife that perished as a result of the spill were as many as 100,000 birds and 1,000 sea otters.

▲ **A pitiful victim of oil pollution, trapped in the thick sludge that has been deposited on the shore. Some lightly affested birds can be cleaned with detergent and saved. This one is too weak and too badly oiled to survive.**

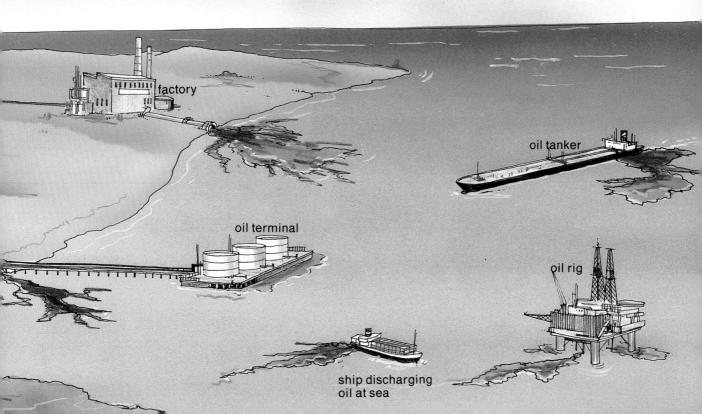

factory

oil tanker

oil terminal

oil rig

ship discharging
oil at sea

▼ Radioactive atoms give out three kinds of radiation from their nucleus. Alpha and beta rays are streams of particles. Gamma rays are a kind of electromagnetic radiation, belonging to the same family as light rays.

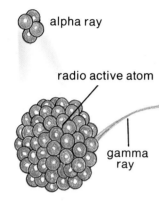

alpha ray

radio active atom

gamma ray

beta ray

Nuclear hazards

About one-twentieth of the world's energy comes from nuclear power stations. There are over 110 of them operating in the United States. These stations extract energy locked up in atoms, specifically the atoms of the heavy metal uranium.

When the nucleus (center) of a uranium atom splits, energy is given out, mainly as heat. At a power station, heat is produced from uranium in a reactor. A coolant (cooling substance) removes the heat, which is used to boil water into steam. The steam is then fed to steam turbines to drive generators to make electricity.

The pros ...

At first sight, nuclear power is attractive. Weight for weight, uranium "fuel" provides 25,000 times as much energy as coal.

Reactors do not produce acid fumes or carbon dioxide and so do not cause the same kind of air pollution as fossil fuels do when they burn.

▼ The worst nuclear accident in the U.S. occurred at the nuclear power station at Three Mile Island in Pennsylvania in March 1979. A faulty pump caused the reactor to overheat. This virtually wrecked the plant and allowed considerable amounts of radiation to escape.

... And the cons

The main problem with nuclear reactors is that they produce waste materials that are highly radioactive. This means that they give out dangerous radiation.

This radiation packs a great deal of energy and will damage living tissue if it enters the body. It gives rise to what is called radiation sickness and, in large enough doses, will cause cancers and death. Even in smaller doses, the radiation can alter the genes in the body cells. This may cause genetic disorders in future generations.

Elaborate precautions and safety measures are therefore taken at nuclear plants to prevent radiation from getting into the environment. Sometimes these measures fail, and radioactive particles escape into the air. They often affect not only the immediate area, but also places downwind, some distance away. They fall to the ground as "fallout" and contaminate the land and growing crops.

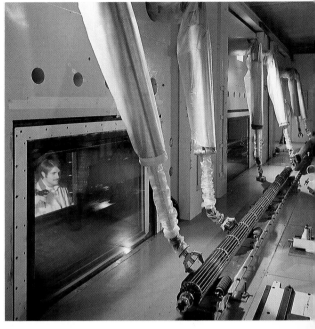

▲ A worker at a nuclear power plant handles fuel rods from a reactor by remote control. The rods are highly radioactive and cannot be handled directly. The handling facility has thick walls and windows to stop radiation escaping into the environment.

Chernobyl

The worst disaster yet to occur at a nuclear power station happened in April 1986 at Chernobyl, near Kiev, in what was then the U.S.S.R. Operating errors at a badly designed nuclear plant caused the uranium core of the reactor to melt and explode. Vast amounts of radioactive materials were blasted into the air.

The fallout from the blast spread over most of Europe, even as far as Sweden. Over 30 people were killed by radiation at the site, and hundreds more suffered radiation sickness. Even seven years later, the countryside for 20 miles (30 km) around Chernobyl was still uninhabitable. Eventually several thousand people throughout Europe may die because of Chernobyl.

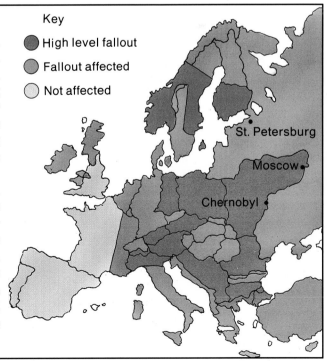

Key
- High level fallout
- Fallout affected
- Not affected

St. Petersburg
Moscow
Chernobyl

3 Conserving the Environment

◄ **Montezuma's Castle is one of a string of national monuments in Arizona. It is named after the famous Aztec emperor Montezuma, but it has nothing to do with him. It is in fact an ancient cliff dwelling, occupied by the Pueblo Indians from about AD 1100 to 1400. As at many national park and monument sites, an informative booklet is available to describe not only the monument, but also the wildlife of the region.**

▼ **In the sunny southwestern states, cars like this will help conserve the environment in the years ahead. They will use the same technology as spacecraft and have panels of cells to make electricity.**

Q **What kind of cells will they be?**

We have discussed in the previous chapters many of the environmental problems that affect our world and what might happen if they get out of hand.

In this chapter we look at some of the steps being taken to conserve the environment – that is, preserve the existing environment, and where possible improve it.

We can improve the environment markedly by reducing our consumption of the fossil fuels. One way we can do this is by making more use of alternative methods of energy production that are friendly to the environment.

Another way we can help the environment is by reducing the vast amounts of waste we throw away. We can do this by recycling – that is, using again – as much of it as possible.

Greater efforts to conserve wildlife are also needed if we are to prevent many species from becoming extinct in the years ahead. One answer might be to establish more national parks, like those in the U.S., where wildlife can flourish under protection.

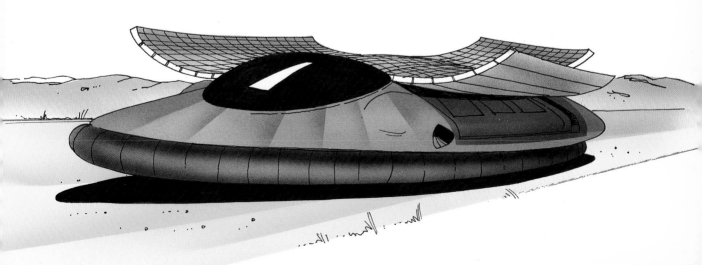

Alternative energy

Most of the energy we use comes from burning the fossil fuels oil, natural gas, and coal. We would help improve the environment immensely if we stopped using them, because they are the cause of most of the pollution that besets our world. One day we will have to do without them anyway because they will run out.

One major source of power that is non-polluting and will never run out is hydroelectricity. This is electricity made by harnessing the power of flowing water. It is what we call a renewable resource: as long as rain continues to fall, hydroelectric power stations will continue to produce electricity – with no pollution.

Harnessing water power is not the only renewable resource nature provides. Other sources are sunshine, the wind, and the heat of the Earth itself.

46

▼ **Many wind turbines cluster together to form what is called a wind farm. Wind farms in California and elsewhere are already producing useful amounts of electricity.**

▶ **This is a solar power tower scheme. Hundreds of mirrors reflect sunlight onto a boiler at the top of a central tower. The concentrated heat boils water into steam to drive turbine-generators that produce electricity.**

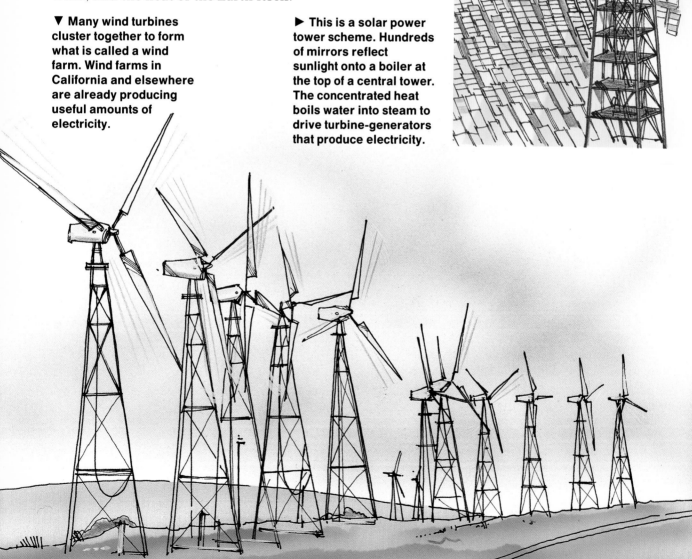

Energy without end – nearly

Even if we do manage to harness more of nature's energy, it will still not be enough to replace the fossil fuels. So scientists are pinning their hopes on developing a method that imitates the method the Sun uses to produce energy. It is called nuclear fusion.

Nuclear fusion is different from nuclear fission, the process today's nuclear power stations use (see page 42). It involves the fusion (joining together) of the nuclei (centers) of atoms of hydrogen. In the fusion process, enormous amounts of heat are given out.

Scientists are carrying out nuclear fusion experiments in powerful machines called tokamaks. Some are using lasers to try to bring about fusion.

Q What other body or bodies in the night sky use nuclear fusion to make their energy: the Moon, the planets Venus, Mars, and Jupiter, the stars, meteors, comets?

▲ This is a geothermal (Earth-heat) power plant in northern California, located in a region of natural geysers. It taps steam from water heated underground and uses it to spin turbine-generators to make electricity.

▼ This is what the power station of the future might look like. It is using sets of powerful lasers to bring about nuclear fusion in a reactor.

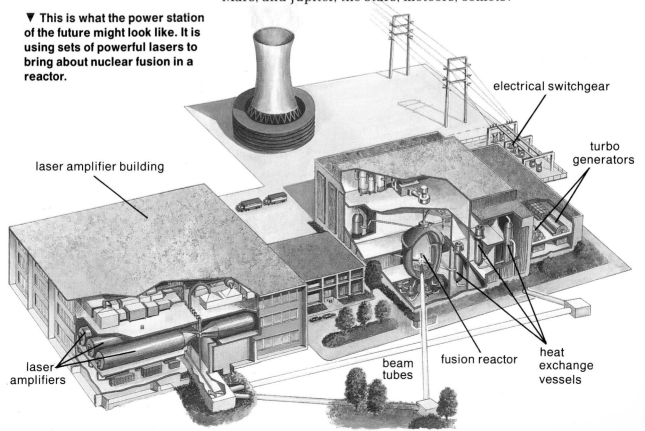

laser amplifier building

electrical switchgear

turbo generators

laser amplifiers

beam tubes

fusion reactor

heat exchange vessels

48

Waste not, want not

This age-old saying will become more and more appropriate as time goes by. Our modern society is very wasteful. On the average in the United States everyone throws away as much as 7 pounds (3 kg) of trash every day. Among the items disposed of every year are over 200 million tires, 2 billion razors and blades, and an incredible 15 billion disposable diapers! The amount of aluminum thrown away in the form of cans and packaging would be enough to build all the aircraft flown by U.S. airlines four times over.

The problem of disposing of these wastes is a headache. Household garbage is commonly burned, and then the ash and solid material are usually dumped on land and buried underneath a layer of soil. But the burning adds to the greenhouse effect and releases poisonous gases into the air. Harmful chemicals can also wash out of the buried garbage and get into drinking water. Rotting organic matter produces methane gas, which adds to the greenhouse effect as well as sometimes catching fire.

▲ Collecting aluminum cans is really worthwhile. This is because extracting metal from its ore takes enormous amounts of electricity. By recycling aluminum, we are saving energy as well as metal. Sometimes it takes more energy to recycle than to process new ore, so care has to be taken to be sure that recycling makes good economic sense. Recycling can sometimes be justified just because it saves on raw material and because were using less landfill that way.

Recycling

Such a wasteful way of living will become unacceptable in the years to come, for it represents a waste of precious raw materials, such as minerals. It also represents a waste of energy – the energy that was used in the first place to process the raw materials into useful products.

Every year we take millions upon millions of tons of minerals from the ground. Soon many of these minerals will be in short supply, especially the mineral ores, from which we get our metals. Early next century we could start running out of some of our most common metals, including copper, gold, silver, tin, zinc, and lead.

The only way we can put off the day when they run out is not to throw them away after we have used them once, but save them and use them again. This is the idea behind recycling. As yet, the U.S. does not recycle as much of its waste as some other countries. It reuses only about one-tenth of its garbage. Japan recycles five times as much, reusing half its waste paper and nearly two-thirds of its glass bottles and food and drink cans. The whole world will have to follow suit in the long run.

Deadly waste

The most dangerous waste materials come from nuclear reactors. Some contain plutonium, one of the deadliest poisons known. It is dangerous, too, because it remains highly radioactive for tens of thousands of years. Such wastes must be buried deep underground and sealed in concrete.

INVESTIGATE

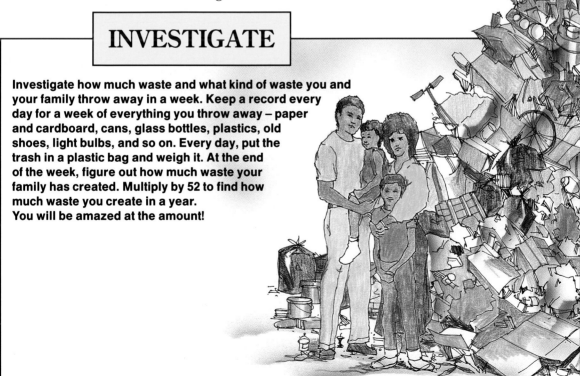

**Investigate how much waste and what kind of waste you and your family throw away in a week. Keep a record every day for a week of everything you throw away – paper and cardboard, cans, glass bottles, plastics, old shoes, light bulbs, and so on. Every day, put the trash in a plastic bag and weigh it. At the end of the week, figure out how much waste your family has created. Multiply by 52 to find how much waste you create in a year.
You will be amazed at the amount!**

Conserving wildlife

In years gone by, there have been mass extinctions of plant and animal species due to some natural catastrophe (see page 20). Today, plants and animals are facing the threat of another mass extinction, but this time because of human activities. As the population increases, more and more land is needed for living space, for farming, and to provide raw materials, such as timber and minerals. These activities threaten wildlife mainly by destroying its habitat.

The destruction of the world's rain forests is especially harmful because they provide the richest habitats on Earth. It is estimated that we may be losing as many as one or two species from these forests every day.

Biodiversity

The pressing need to prevent this wholesale destruction of species led to the Biodiversity Convention, signed by many nations at the Earth Summit in Rio de Janeiro, Brazil, in June 1992. Basically, the idea behind the Convention is to provide money to help countries preserve their unique species of plants and animals, and manage them as a valuable natural resource.

▼ The Monterey pine is an evergreen originally found only here, on the Monterey Peninsula in California. A species like this, found only in a limited area, is often at risk of extinction. Fortunately, this is not the case with the Monterey pine. It has been successfully planted elsewhere in the U.S. and as far away as New Zealand.

Save the whales, rhino, elephant, gorilla, panda ...

Another human activity that threatens animal species is hunting. Humans have always hunted for food and, more recently, for sport. But hunting in one form or another has brought many species to the edge of extinction.

Whales the intelligent mammals of the sea, were until the early 1980's being slaughtered at the rate of some 60,000 a year. Thankfully, in 1986 a whaling ban came into effect, following pressure from such bodies as the World Wildlife Fund, and environmental action groups such as Greenpeace.

Such bodies have been successful in alerting public opinion around the world to other species at risk and to environmental problems in general. Among other highly endangered species is the rhinoceros in Africa. It is protected, but is still being killed by poachers just for its horns, which some believe have magical properties. Elephants are also being slaughtered for their tusks, which are used for making ivory ornaments.

Other species are at risk because they are being taken from the wild to be sold as pets – the beautiful Golden marmoset of South America is an example. International agreements restrict the trade of wild animals, but they are often difficult to enforce. The main agreement is CITES, the Convention on International Trade in Endangered Species. This also covers trade in plants.

Some of the successes in wildlife conservation. The Arabian oryx was successfully bred in captivity after becoming extinct in the wild and has been reintroduced to Saudi Arabia under protection. The Bengal tiger is now heavily protected in nine reserves in India as a result of a program called Project Tiger. Numbers of sperm whales are gradually recovering, following an international whaling ban in 1986.

U.S. National Parks and Monuments

The United States is exceptionally rich in natural, and man-made wonders. Most of the outstanding sites are now cared for by the National Park Service.

President Woodrow Wilson signed the National Park Service Act in August 1916: "To conserve the scenery and the natural and historic objects and the wildlife therein and to provide for the enjoyment of the same ... unimpaired for the enjoyment of future generations."

The National Park Service now manages over 350 sites throughout the U.S. These sites cover some 80 million acres (32 million hectares). The most important sites, as far as the environment is concerned, are the national parks and monuments. A map showing parks and monuments in the U.S. is shown on pages 54 and 55.

52

▼ **Walnut Canyon National Monument, Arizona.**
The remains of dwellings lived in by people called the Sinagua ("without water"), between about AD 1125 and 1250. Anthropologists reckon that their descendants live today among the Hopi Indians.

▼ **Yellowstone National Park.**
The first national park, Yellowstone, in Wyoming, is still one of the most popular. It is a wilderness inhabited by grizzlies, elk, moose, and buffalo. But it is best known for its geysers and hot springs.

Q One famous geyser performs almost hourly, spurting 35,000 gallons of water 100 feet (30 meters) into the air. What is it called?

◀ **Yosemite National Park, California.**
The Park abounds in spectacular scenery like this. It is centered on Yosemite Valley, which is encircled by sheer granite cliffs. The area was designated a state park in 1864, becoming a national park in 1890.

▶ **Sunset Crater National Monument, Arizona.**
Part of the slope rising up to Sunset Crater, created by a volcano that erupted in about AD 1065. Lava-flows and thick layers of cinders cover the surrounding landscape.

National parks are concerned with the upkeep and preservation of outstanding natural features, such as the Grand Canyon, and the provision of facilities for recreation. National monuments include not only natural features, but also sites of prehistoric and historic importance, such as Montezuma's Castle (see page 44).

The greatest concentration of national parks and monuments occurs in the western states, which have some of the most spectacular scenery on Earth. Wyoming boasts the nation's first national park, Yellowstone, which was established in 1872.

The splendid canyon and desert landscapes of the western parks contrasts markedly with the verdant expanses of the few parks in the east, such as the Shenandoah National Park in northern Virginia and the Big Cypress and Everglades National Parks in Florida.

Alaska

Hawaii

This map shows the location of the national parks and national monuments in the United States. The parks and monuments are under the care and protection of the National Park Service.

Monuments

1. John Day Fossil Beds
2. Custer Battlefeild
3. Devils Tower
4. Jewel Cave
5. Craters of the Moon
6. Hagerman Fossil Beds
7. Oregon Caves
8. Lava Beds
9. Fossil Butte
10. Agate Fossil Beds
11. Scotts Bluff
12. Muir Woods
13. Pinnacles
14. Timpanogos Cave
15. Dinosaur
16. Colorado
17. Black Canyon of the Gunnison
18. Florissant Fossil Beds
19. Great Sand Dunes
20. Yucca House
21. Hovenweep
22. Natural Bridges
23. Rainbow Bridge
24. Pipe Spring
25. Cedar Breaks
26. Death Valley
27. Navajo
28. Aztec Ruins
29. Capulin Volcano
30. Sunset Crater Volcano
31. Wupatki
32. Bandelier
33. Fort Union
34. Walnut Canyon
35. Tuzigoot
36. Montezuma Castle
37. El Moro
38. El Malpais
39. Petroglyph
40. Salinas Pueblo Missions
41. Joshua Tree
42. Tonto
43. Gila Cliff Dwellings
44. White Sands
45. Cabrillo
46. Hohokam Pima
47. Casa Grande
48. Organ Pipe Cactus
49. Saguaro
50. Chircahua
51. Pipestone
52. Effigy Mounds
53. Fort Stanwix
54. Mound City Group
55. Fort McHenry
56. George Washington birthplace
57. Booker T. Washington
58. George Washington Carver
59. Russell Cave
60. Congaree Swamp
61. Fort Sumter
62. Poverty Point
63. Ocmulgee
64. Fort Pulaski
65. Fort Frederica
66. Castillo de San Marcos
67. Fort Matanzas

Park or preserve

1. Olympic
2. North Cascades
3. Mount Rainier
4. Glacier
5. Theodore Roosevelt
6. Theodore Roosevelt
7. Crater Lake
8. Redwood
9. Yellowstone
10. Grand Teton
11. Badlands
12. Wind Cave
13. Lassen Volcanic
14. Great Basin
15. Rocky Mountain
16. Yosemite
17. Kings Canyon
18. Sequoia
19. Arches
20. Capitol Reef
21. Canyonlands
22. Bryce Canyon
23. Zion
24. Grand Canyon
25. Channel Islands
26. Big Bend
27. Voyageurs
28. Isle Royale
29. Acadia
30. Shenandoah
31. Mammoth Cave
32. Great Smoky Mountains
33. Hot Springs
34. Big Cypress
35. Everglades
36. Biscayne

Alaska

1. Noatak
2. Gates of the Arctic
3. Kobuk Valley
4. Bering Land Bridge
5. Yukon-Charley Rivers
6. Denali
7. Lake Clark
8. Wrangell-St. Ellis
9. Glacier Bay
10. Katmai

Hawaii

1. Haleakala
2. Hawaii Volcanoes

Milestones

1681 On the island of Mauritius, in the Indian Ocean, the turkey-size bird the dodo became extinct as a result of hunting.

1906 President Theodore Roosevelt established the first national monument, Devils Tower in Wyoming.

1916 President Woodrow Wilson signed the Act bringing the National Parks Service into being.

1979 An accident at the nuclear power station at Three Mile Island in Pennsylvania threatened to cause a meltdown of the core. Had this happened, dangerous amounts of radioactivity would have been released and harmed thousands of people.

1980 Mt. St Helens, a volcanic peak in the Cascades mountain range in Washington State, erupted, blasting away the top 1,300 feet (400 meters) of its crest. The blast and ash fall devastated some 200 square miles (500 square kilometers) of the surrounding countryside. In all some 400 million tons (360 million tonnes) of material were ejected into the atmosphere by the eruption.

1985 Spacecraft confirmed that the ozone layer over the continent of Antarctica was noticeably thinning, giving rise to the concept of the "ozone hole."

1986 A combination of operator error and bad design led to an explosion at a nuclear power station at Chernobyl in the Ukraine, then part of the Soviet Union. Massive doses of radiation escaped into the environment, subsequently spreading over much of Europe. Over 30 people were killed and hundreds more affected by radiation sickness.

The International Whaling Commission banned the commercial hunting of whales, but allowed the killing of limited numbers for scientific purposes.

1987 Twenty-four nations signed the Montreal Protocol agreeing to reduce production of CFCs, the gases mainly responsible for ozone destruction.

1989 The tanker *Exxon Valdez* ran aground on the coast of Alaska, with a devastating impact on the environment. Killer whales, seals, and otters were among the wildlife that suffered badly. An estimated half a million seabirds died.

1991 Retreating Iraqi troops blew up and set fire to some 600 oilwells in Kuwait during the Gulf War, with a disastrous effect on the environment.

In the Philippines in South-east Asia, the volcano Mt. Pinatubo erupted, pouring out huge volumes of ash and dust, causing destructive mud slides that destroyed or damaged 1000,000 homes. Dust rising into the high atmosphere led to a significant cooling of the Earth's climate.

1992 A "World Summit to save the Earth" was held in Rio de Janeiro, capital city of Brazil in South America. Attended by more than a hundred world leaders, it produced a 600-page agenda for saving our planet, addressing the problems of global warming, ozone depletion, and the necessity to preserve biological diversity, and prevent the destruction of species and their habitats.

56

Glossary

ACID RAIN Rain containing acid, which forms when acidic gases are released into the air by burning fuels.

ANTARCTIC The very cold region around the South Pole.

ARCTIC The very cold region around the North Pole.

CAMOUFLAGE The pattern, color, or shape of an animal that enables it to blend in with its surroundings, and hide from predators or prey.

CARBON DIOXIDE A gas formed when fuels burn in the air; it is the main gas that is causing the greenhouse effect.

CEREALS Crops that belong to the grass family that produce ears or cobs of grain. The main cereals include wheat, corn, rice, millet, rye, oats, and barley

CFCS Chemicals containing chlorine that are attacking the ozone layer in the atmosphere.

COMMUNITY All the animals and plants that live in the same habitat.

CONIFER TREES Ones that bear their seeds in cones. They are usually evergreen and have needle-like leaves.

CONTINENTAL DRIFT The gradual movement of the continents across the face of the Earth.

DECIDUOUS TREES Ones that shed all their leaves at once, usually in the fall.

DESERT A region that has little, if any, rainfall during the year. Most deserts are very hot, but some are very cold.

EARTHQUAKE The shaking of the ground, due to the sudden movement of sections of the Earth's crust.

ECOLOGY The study of animals and plants, and the environment in which they live.

ENDANGERED SPECIES Those in danger of becoming extinct.

ENVIRONMENT The surroundings, both the physical (rocks, air, climate) and the living (plants, animals).

EQUATOR An imaginary line around the Earth midway between the North and South Poles.

EROSION The gradual wearing away of rocks due to the action of running water, the weather, and so on.

EXTINCTION The dying out of a living species.

FALLOUT The radioactive material that falls back to Earth after it has been released in a nuclear accident or after the explosion of a nuclear weapon.

FERTILIZER Material added to the ground to make it more fertile and help plants grow well.

FOOD CHAIN The system in which an animal eats food but becomes food for another, which becomes food for yet another, and so on.

FOOD WEB The combination of several interrelated food chains.

FOSSIL The remains of a once-living thing, plant or animal.

FOSSIL FUELS Coal, oil, and natural gas, fuels that are the remains of plants and animals that lived long, long ago.

FUNGICIDE A chemical that kills fungus diseases, such as mildew.

GEOTHERMAL ENERGY Heat that comes from the Earth, for example, from geysers.

GLACIER A "river of ice," a frozen mass of ice that is slowly moving.

GLOBAL WARMING The warming up of the Earth that occurs because of the greenhouse effect.

GREENHOUSE EFFECT The way the atmosphere acts like a greenhouse and traps the Sun's heat.

HABITAT The natural surroundings in which a plant or animal lives.

HYDROELECTRICITY Electricity produced by harnessing the power of running water.

INSECTICIDE A chemical that kills insects.

METHANE One of the "greenhouse gases" in the atmosphere. Livestock are a major source of the gas.

MINERAL A chemical substance found in the ground.

NATIONAL PARK A region of land in which development for settlement, industry, and mining is banned, and in which wildlife is strictly protected.

NUCLEAR REACTION A process in which the nuclei (centers) of atoms split apart (nuclear fission) or join together (nuclear fusion), releasing enormous amounts of energy.

OZONE A different form of oxygen, whose particles are made up of three, not two, atoms. A layer of ozone in the atmosphere filters out dangerous rays from the Sun.

OZONE HOLE A noticeable thinning of the ozone layer, caused mainly by the presence of CFCs in the atmosphere.

PHOTOSYNTHESIS The process by which green plants make their food, by chemically combining carbon dioxide and water in the presence of sunlight, which provides the energy for the process.

POLLUTION The poisoning of the environment – the land, the sea, and the air.

ORE A mineral from which metal can be extracted.

PERMAFROST Permanently frozen ground that occurs in polar regions.

PESTICIDE A chemical that kills pests.

PREDATOR An animal that hunts other animals for food.

PREY An animal that is hunted for food.

RADIOACTIVE Giving out dangerous radiation.

RAIN FOREST A thick forest of broad-leaved trees that grows in tropical regions. Rain forests are exceptionally rich in wildlife.

REACTOR The unit in a nuclear power station in which the nuclear reactions take place.

RECYCLING Using something again after it has been used once.

SMOG A smoky fog that forms in some cities when polluted air gets trapped.

SOLAR ENERGY Energy from the Sun.

SPECIES In general, species means kind. But more specifically, Species is the division in animal classification below Genus. Scientifically, an animal (or a plant) is named by its genus and species. For example, the scientific name for the endangered Indian rhinoceros is *Rhinoceros unicornis*.

SULFUR DIOXIDE One of the main polluting gases responsible for causing acid rain. It escapes into the environment from the chimneys of power stations and factories.

TORNADO A highly destructive wind storm in which winds spin round at speeds of up to 300 mph (500 km/h).

TROPICS A region with a hot climate on either side of the Equator. Strictly speaking, it is the region between latitude 23½° North (the Tropic of Cancer) and latitude 23½° South (the Tropic of Capricorn).

ULTRAVIOLET RAYS Rays given out by the Sun, which tan the skin but which can also burn and cause skin cancer. The ozone layer in the atmosphere prevents much of the radiation from reaching ground level.

WEATHERING The gradual wearing away of rocks by the action of the weather.

WETLANDS Regions where water lays on the surface for most of the time, such as estuaries, mud flats, and swamps.

WIND FARM A large group of wind turbines that produce electricity by harnessing the energy blowing in the wind.

Answers

Page 9

1. The flow would be greater in May because the snow in the mountains would have melted. The flow would probably be less in September after a dry Californian summer.

2. Beavers build dams to raise the water level of the pond when they build their lodge. This is to make the entrance to the lodge underwater. This helps protect it from land predators.

Page 10

Water is H-2-O, or as it should properly be written H_2O, which is the correct chemical formula for water. The formula indicates that in the water molecule two hydrogen atoms are combined with one oxygen atom.

Page 13

We call this "river of ice" a glacier. Some glaciers in Alaska travel up to 60 feet (18 meters) a day during the summer.

Page 14

The proper name for the violent windstorm nicknamed a twister is a tornado.

Page 17

Bees and other insects visit flowers to sip their nectar. As they do so, pollen from the flower falls on their bodies, which they then carry on to other flowers. This transfer of pollen, or pollination, fertilizes the flowers so that they can produce seeds and therefore reproduce themselves.

▲ Bees are among the main pollinators of flowers, carrying pollen from plant to plant. They also collect pollen for food. They collect the pollen on so-called pollen baskets on their hind legs and carry it back to the hive to feed the grub-like larvae.

Page 24

With 10 babies born every 4 seconds, 78,840,000 are born every year. In a leap year, of course, the total jumps another 216,000.

Page 26

66 billion tons (60 billion tonnes) of wheat are produced in the world each year.

Page 30

The amount of copper ore mined on average per day in the 86 years between 1906 and 1992 is (to the nearest 1,000 tons/tonnes) 111,000 tons (101,000 tonnes). Remember to allow for leap years!

Page 35

Lakes are especially affected by acid rain because they are enclosed bodies of water. The acid therefore builds up. To overcome the acidity of some lakes, chalk or limestone is added to them.

Investigation

Adding vinegar to powdered chalk (not blackboard chalk) makes the chalk fizz and give off bubbles of gas. The vinegar is attacking the chalk because it is an acid. Acid rain attacks limestone, which is chemically the same as chalk, in the same way.

Page 36

Workout

The cattle give off nearly 274 billion pounds, or 137 million tons (124 million tonnes), in a year.

Page 38

1. X-rays are used in hospitals to "see" inside the body. X-ray photographs show up broken bones, for example.

2. If the picture were drawn to scale, the edge of the atmosphere would be very close to the surface of the Earth.

Page 40

Animals higher up the food chain prey on animals lower down. The chemical poisons build up in animals lower down, so when the animals higher up feed on them they get a concentrated dose of poison.

Page 45

They will be panels of solar cells, which harness the energy in sunlight and convert it to electricity.

Page 47

The stars – and the Sun – use nuclear fusion to generate the energy to keep them shining. The other bodies – the Moon, the planets, meteors, and comets – do not produce light of their own. They shine in the night sky because they reflect sunlight.

Page 53

The famous geyser is called "Old Faithful."

61

For further reading

Blashfield, Jean F. and Black, Wallace B.
Recycling.
Childrens Press, Chicago. 1991.

Goldberg, Jake.
Economics and the Environment.
Chelsea House. New York. 1993.

Herda, D. J.
Environmental America: The North Central States.
Willbrook Press. 1991.

Koral, April.
Our Global Greenhouse.
Franklin Watts. New York. 1991.

Markham, Adam.
The Environment.
Rourke. Vero Beach. FL. 1988.

Miles, Betty.
Save the Earth: An Action Handbook for Kids.
Knopf. New York. 1991.

Pringle, Laurence.
Global Warming: Assessing the Greenhouse Threat.
Arcade Publishers. New York. 1990.

Schwartz, Meryl.
The Environment and the Law.
Chelsea House. New York. 1990.

Tesar, Jenny E.
Global Warming.
Facts on File. New York. 1991.

Waid, Mike.
What You Can Do For the Environment.
Chelsea House. New York. 1993.

Index